Nicholas M

SOPHIE'S CHOICE

OPERA IN FOUR ACTS

Libretto by the composer
based on the novel by
William Styron

FABER *ff* MUSIC

Commissioned by the British Broadcasting Corporation in association with
the Royal Opera House, Covent Garden

© 2002 by Faber Music Ltd
First published in 2002 by Faber Music Ltd
3 Queen Square London WC1N 3AU
Printed in England by Caligraving Ltd

ISBN 0-571-52126-6

Full score and parts available on hire

To buy Faber Music publications or to find out about the full range of titles available
please contact your local music retailer or Faber Music sales enquiries:

Faber Music Limited, Burnt Mill, Elizabeth Way, Harlow, CM20 2HX England
Tel: +44 (0)1279 82 89 82   Fax: +44 (0)1279 82 89 83
sales@fabermusic.com   www.fabermusic.com

CHARACTERS

NARRATOR   Bass-baritone
Writer. In his mid to late fifties.

SOPHIE (SOFIA) ZAWISTOWSKA   Mezzo-soprano
Polish refugee immigrant to the United States. Now working as a secretary-receptionist to a doctor. Aged thirty two.

NATHAN LANDAU   High baritone
Employed by a pharmaceutical company. Aged twenty nine.

STINGO   Tenor
Aspiring writer. Aged twenty two.

YETTA ZIMMERMAN   Contralto
Widow. Owner of a boarding house in Brooklyn. Aged about sixty.

ZBIGNIEW BIEGANSKI   Bass-baritone
Sophie's father. Professor of Jurisprudence at the University of Cracow. Aged about fifty five.

RUDOLPH FRANZ HÖSS   Dramatic Tenor
Obersturmbannführer. Commandant of Auschwitz-Birkenau concentration camp. Aged forty three.

DOCTOR   Baritone
Hauptsturmführer. Camp doctor at Auschwitz. In his late thirties.

WANDA   Soprano
Leader in Polish resistance movement. About thirty years old.

LARRY LANDAU   Baritone
Nathan's elder brother. Doctor. Aged around forty.

LIBRARIAN   Baritone

BARTENDER   Baritone

OLD WOMAN IN TRAIN   Contralto

YOUNG MAN IN TRAIN   Tenor

JAN *Sophie's son. Ten years old.*   Non-singing role

EVA *Sophie's daughter. Eight years old.*   Non-singing role

CHORUS OF PRISONERS, BAR PATRONS   SATB

CAMP GUARDS, etc.   Non-singing roles

PLACE AND TIME OF THE ACTION

The scenes in Brooklyn, Forest Hills and Washington in 1947 run chronologically through summer and early autumn of that year.

ACT I

SCENE 1   A boarding house in Brooklyn, New York; summer 1947

SCENE 2   A college library; 1946

SCENE 3   Sophie's room in the boarding house; later the same day

SCENE 4   Stingo's room in the boarding house; summer 1947

ACT II

SCENE 1   The boarding house; the following morning

SCENE 2   Stingo's room in the boarding house; summer 1947;
and Professor Bieganski's study in Cracow, Poland; December 1938

SCENE 3   Sophie's room in the boarding house; summer 1947

ACT III

SCENE 1   Warsaw, Poland; March 1943

SCENE 2   A rail car, Poland; March 1943

SCENE 3   Auschwitz-Birkenau concentration camp, Oswiecim, Poland;
the camp Commandant's office; October 1943

SCENE 4   The Maple Court Lounge, Brooklyn; early autumn 1947

ACT IV

SCENE 1   The apartment of Larry Landau, Forest Hills, NY; early autumn 1947

SCENE 2   The boarding house, Brooklyn; later the same day

SCENE 3   A hotel room in Washington DC; early autumn 1947

SCENE 4   The rail station at Auschwitz-Birkenau; April 1, 1943

SCENE 5   The hotel room in Washington

SCENE 6   The boarding house, Brooklyn; afternoon of the next day

CONTENTS

ACT I

Prologue

(The Narrator appears…)

NARRATOR It was the early summer of nineteen forty seven.
I vividly remember that year,
sunny and mild, flower fragrant…

I was twenty two,
and had come up to New York from the South,
hoping to become a writer.
I yearned passionately to produce the novel
so long captive in my mind.

One fine day in June
I walked down a Brooklyn street
lined with greening sycamores,
and took a room in the boarding house
of Mrs. Yetta Zimmerman.

(We see Yetta Zimmerman's boarding house in Brooklyn; summer 1947. To one side, occupying the lesser part of the stage, Stingo's room with door out to the hallway. The furnishings are rather sparse; visible items include a worktable-desk with typewriter, an armchair, and some well stocked bookshelves. In the hallway outside, stairs lead up to the floor above where Nathan's room is located. A door on the other side of the hallway leads to Sophie's room, which occupies the larger part of the stage. At the back of the hallway is the street door. It is late afternoon. Stingo is at work in his room.)

So it was I came to know
Sophie and Nathan…

Scene 1

(The novel Stingo is working on is proceeding with difficulty. He rises restlessly from his chair, strolls to look out of the window, takes a book down from the shelves. As he paces about the room he becomes aware of a furious quarrel taking place on the floor above.)

NATHAN *(invisible, from the back of the upper floor)*
 Don't give me any of *that*, you hear?
 You're a liar, a miserable lying whore!

SOPHIE Nathan, *listen*…

NATHAN A two-timing, double crossing whore!
 Spreading those legs of yours
 for a cheap, chiselling quack doctor.
 Oh *God*! Let me get out of here before I *murder* you!
(Sophie and Nathan appear at the top of the stairway, he in the throes of an explosive and bitter rage, she tearful and pleading.)
 You were *born* a whore and you'll *die* a whore!

SOPHIE *(sobbing)*
 Nathan! Nathan! You must listen, *please*.

NATHAN *(bellowing)*
 Don't you understand?
 You fill me with *in*-fin-ite revulsion,
 pure un-a-*dul*-ter-a-ted loathing!

(He plunges down the stairs, Sophie following.)

SOPHIE   Nathan, don't go! I need you, Nathan.
              You need *me. Don't* go!

NATHAN   *Me* need *you*?
              I need you like any goddamned insufferable *disease* I could mention.
              Like a case of *anthrax*, hear me?
              Like trichinosis! Pellagra! Encephalitis!
              Cancer of the brain, for Christ's sake!
              (howling dementedly) Aaaahooo-o!
              I need you like *death! DEATH!*

(Stingo has come to the door of his room and looks on with bewilderment.)

SOPHIE   Nathan, *please!*... Where are you going?

NATHAN   *Going*? I'm going to clear out of *this* place.
              Then I'm going to tell the Immigration Service
              they'd better ship you back to Poland
              for peddling your ass to any doctor in Brooklyn
              who needs a quick lay.
              (chuckling with satisfaction)
              Back to Cracow, baby!

(He lunges for the street door, and in doing so brushes up against Stingo.)
              (with oily sarcasm)
              Well, lookee who's here,
              our new roomer from the South.
              Why, that's just what we need in this house,
              a good ol' Southerner to fit in with all the other funnies.
              Too bad I won't be around for some lively conversation;
              we'd have had great fun, shootin' the breeze, you and I.
              We could have talked about all those *Southern* sports,
              like lynching niggers – or *coons*, I think you call them.
              Or maybe enjoyed some Southern *culture*;
              sittin' around listening to hillbilly records.
              Ah well, too bad. Old Nathan's got to hit the road.
              (suddenly clasping Stingo's hand)
              So long, Cracker. See you in another life!

(He plunges out of the street door. Sophie weeps miserably. Stingo doesn't know what to say. He pulls out a handkerchief and silently hands it to Sophie.)

SOPHIE   Oh, I love him so much... so much!
              I love him so much I'll *die* without him.
              (dabbing her eyes)
              He has crazy idea I'm making love to my employer, the doctor.
              It's so unfair of him – to say *that*!
              I was never unfaithful to Nathan, never!
              He's the only man I've ever made love to,
              except my husband – and my husband's dead!
              What am I going to do? I love him so...

STINGO   Come and sit down.

SOPHIE   Thank you.

(He leads her to a chair in his room.)

STINGO   Oh boy – that Nathan!
              I've never seen anything like him in my life.
              He can certainly dole out the insults.
              'Cracker' indeed!

| | And what about that bit about lynching |
| | and all that crap about the South? |

SOPHIE   I'm sorry, Stingo, he shouldn't say those awful things to you.
           He doesn't really mean it.

STINGO   How can he talk like that to *anyone*?
           If you ask me, you're well rid of him.

SOPHIE   Oh, you know, he's right about so much.
           Not about I wasn't faithful – I've been faithful to him always.
           But other things. Like when he said I didn't dress right,
           or when he said I was sloppy and didn't clean up.
           Then he called me a dirty Polack,
           and I knew, yes I knew, I deserved it.
           Or when he took me to these nice restaurants
           and I always keeped...

(She looks enquiringly at Stingo.)

STINGO   Kept...

SOPHIE   I always kept the *carte* – I mean, the menu – for a souvenir.
           He said I was stealing; menus cost money.
           He was right, you know.

STINGO   It hardly seems like grand larceny.

SOPHIE   No, I done so many things that were wrong.
           Maybe I deserve it, that he leave me.
           But I was *never* unfaithful to him, never!
           I love Nathan from the first moment I meet him...

(The scene fades...)

Interlude

(The Narrator appears...)

NARRATOR   At the time, though feeling ill and weak,
           Sophie was attending English classes.
           There she had been captured
           by the music of an American poet,
           the name half-heard, misapprehended...

Scene 2

(A college library, the previous year. The Librarian is seated behind a counter. Nathan is at a nearby bookstack, idly turning the pages of a book. Sophie enters. She is pale, and walks slowly.)

SOPHIE   Excuse me, please, where I find catalogue file
           of list of works by American poet Emil Dickens?

LIBRARIAN *(brusquely)*
           In the catalogue room, first door to the left.
           But you won't find any such listing.

SOPHIE   Won't find any such listing? Why is that, please?

(The Librarian stares at her stonily.)

LIBRARIAN   *Charles* Dickens is an *English* writer.
              There is *no* American poet by the name of Dickens.

(Sophie begins to feel dizzy. She holds on to the counter top.)

SOPHIE   … I'm *sure* there is an American poet Dickens…

(She is swept by a wave of nausea and staggers a little.)

LIBRARIAN *(with mounting hostility)*
              Listen, I am *telling* you, do you *hear* me?
              There is *no such person*!
              You want me to draw you a *picture*?

(Sophie suddenly faints and slumps to the floor. Nathan, who has witnessed the whole scene, comes over quickly and attends solicitously to her.)

NATHAN   Don't move now, you just had a funny little spell.
              Don't worry about anything.
(He turns on the Librarian.)
              You *schmuck*! This nice and lovely girl here
              has a little trouble with the language,
              and you treat her like some piece of *dreck* walked in!
              Can't you see she's a foreigner, you filthy *momzer*!
              You've as much business around books as a plumber!
(The Librarian reddens and hurries off into the adjoining bookstacks. Nathan assists Sophie to a seat.)
              Just be still, now.
              Let the doctor take care of everything.
(He arranges a cushion behind her head.)
              There, rest your head back.
              Ah, but you're so *beautiful*.
              How did you get to be so beautiful?

SOPHIE   I suddenly felt so bad –
              I thought I'm going to die…

NATHAN   No, you're *not* going to die, you'll live to be a hundred.
              Pulse is steady, you'll be fine.
              Here, try this little sip of water.
(He holds the water to her lips.)
              What's your name, sweetie?
              No – don't tell me now, just lie still and look beautiful.
              You're going to be all well in just a minute…

(Nathan continues to minister to Sophie as the scene fades…)

Interlude

(The Narrator appears…)

NARRATOR   Nathan once told me
              his meeting with Sophie was 'cinematic'.
              It happened in the delightful and haphazard way
              of Hollywood daydreams.
              Sophie for her part,
              most deeply and indelibly remembered
              Nathan's awesome tenderness…

Scene 3

(Sophie's room in the boarding house. The modest but comfortable furnishings include a bed, several chairs, a dressing table, a side table with phonograph and stack of records, and a shelf of books on the wall. One part of the room serves as a kitchen area. To one side a table set for dinner, with candles and wine glasses. It is early evening of the same day. Nathan, busying himself about the room, is in the middle of preparing a meal. Sophie is lying on the bed with a pillow behind her head. She wakes...)

NATHAN   How do you feel?

SOPHIE   Better, much better.

NATHAN   Good. I'll bet you have a severe deficiency anaemia,
that's why you passed out.
Baby, have you been eating properly?

SOPHIE   Much better than all my life, I swear.
I can't eat much fat of animals, but all else is okay.

NATHAN   Bound to be a deficiency of iron.
You could have fallen behind with it
and never had a chance to catch up.
It's a very simple thing to cure.
We've got to get you fixed up.
You can't run around Brooklyn fainting in libraries
and scaring people half to death.

SOPHIE   I don't know why, I suddenly felt so ill and weak.

NATHAN *(jocularly)*
The doctor thinks you need a big pill
to try to bring some colour into that beautiful white skin.
(normal voice)
I'm going to take you to see my brother. Okay?
My brother's a doctor, one of the best there is.
He can help you.

SOPHIE   But you... I thought...

NATHAN   You thought I was a doctor? No, I'm a biologist.
I work for a pharmaceutical company here in Brooklyn.
While you were sleeping I bought a few things for dinner.
(He searches for items in a grocery bag.)
(with heavy Jewish accent)
Oy vey! Vot a *mishegoss*...
(Sophie giggles.)
You know, I haven't the faintest notion of
who you are or what you do.

SOPHIE   I'm a receptionist.
I work for a doctor, a chiropractor.
(Nathan groans disapprovingly.)
He's a very nice man... What you call a *mensh.*

NATHAN   *Mensh, shmensh,* a girl like you working for some *humbug* –

SOPHIE   I was the only job I could *get*, when I came here.

NATHAN   Of course. I'm sorry.

SOPHIE   I have no talents, you see.
I begun an education a long time ago.

It was never finished.
I wished to become a teacher of music, but it was impossible.
I'm a very incomplete person.

NATHAN *(indicating the shelf of books)*
Well, I see your education continues.
By the way, that American poet you were looking for –
the name is Emily Dickinson.

> 'Because I could not stop for Death,
> He kindly stopped for me;
> The carriage held but just ourselves
> And Immortality.

> We slowly drove, he knew no haste,
> And I had put away
> My labour, and my leisure too,
> For his civility.

> Since then 'tis centuries; but each
> Feels shorter than the day
> I first surmised the horses' heads
> Were toward eternity.'

SOPHIE   A beautiful poem...

(Nathan glances pointedly at the tattooed number on Sophie's arm.)

NATHAN   Tell me, you're not Jewish, are you?

SOPHIE *(hastily withdrawing her arm)*
No. Do I seem so?

NATHAN   At first guess I just assumed you were.
Then I thought, Danish, or maybe Finnish –
those Slavic cheekbones!
(indicating the books again)
But these are all Polish –
so it seems you're a beautiful Polack!
A Polish lady...

SOPHIE   *Pas de flatterie, monsieur...*

NATHAN *(examining the books more closely)*
These are all translations, I see.
American writers: Hemingway, Wolfe, Dreiser.
Why nothing from your own country?

SOPHIE   I have nothing left from that time. I lost everything.
After the war, when I came to America, I begin my life again.
All you see in this room is new – books, clothes, everything.
It's all part of my new life.

NATHAN   And what of your old life before you came here?

SOPHIE   I grew up in the beautiful city of Cracow;
it was there I spent my early life.
Those were good years for my family and me,
and good for our country, too.
'Sunny times for Poland', my father used to say.

Here, in this bright new world,
my thoughts often return to that peaceful old city.

How far away it all seems now;
a dream of childhood, an idyll of sweet content.
Our old house was quiet and full of shadows;
it seemed so warm, so safe.
How I loved that house! At night, waiting for sleep,
I lay in the dark of my room high under the eaves,
while the gentle sounds of evening
floated through the open window:
footsteps, voices in the narrow street,
the clock tower striking in the square.
Far below, I heard my mother play the piano.
The music rose up through the house, faint and beautiful,
passing through my dreamy mind and lulling me to sleep.

I was the beloved only child of my parents.
What wonderful people they were! –
my father a professor of law, my mother a teacher of music.
I spent many happy hours with my mother
preparing fine meals for our friends
or playing duets at the piano.
What a fine life, I thought, to play beautiful music
and be married to a man like my father!

Later, I married Casimir Zawistowski, a disciple of my father.
At the time I was still very young,
but I was so happy with Casimir,
and loved him very much.
He was tender and generous, and so intelligent!
You see, I am attracted only to intelligent men…
(She breaks off, embarrassed by her ingenuous remark.)
I feel quite rested now, even a little hungry.

NATHAN   Good! Dinner will soon be ready.

(Sophie makes a move to get up.)

SOPHIE   Please, let me help –

NATHAN *(restraining her)*
No! Sit down – quit fussing around!
Please, just let Nathan take charge – this is *my* show!
(Nathan chatters away while finishing the dinner preparations.)
It's plain as the nose
on your pretty but incredibly pale face
that what you need is iron –
massive infusions of iron.
Yes, massive infusions of iron!
So tonight's dinner is *loaded* with it!
On the menu is calf's liver –
Nothing is better than liver.
And leeks – *filled* with iron!
Liver with onions is standard, of course,
but with leeks, sweetiepie,
it becomes something special.
They'll also improve the timbre of your voice.
Did you know the Emperor Nero
used to eat leeks every day
to deepen the sound of his voice,
and so he could croon

while he had Seneca drawn and quartered?
Yes, I've decided that what you need is iron,
iron, iron, iron – *iron*!
And that's why we're also going to have
creamed spinach and a plain little salad.

(He produces a bottle of wine.)

And to complement our little repast –
Chateaux Margaux, nineteen thirty seven –
the last great pre-war vintage.

SOPHIE   How wonderful!...

(Nathan hands Sophie a glass.)

NATHAN   *Santé!*

(They drink.)

SOPHIE   Mmm... delicious!

NATHAN   Madame, if you will – *à table!*

(As they sit down to dinner the scene gradually dims.)

Scene 4

(Stingo's room in the boarding house, somewhat later than Scene 1. Sophie and Stingo are still in conversation.)

SOPHIE   So you see, Stingo, how Nathan saved my life.
Here I was, very ill, fainting, falling down,
and along comes this sweet and gentle man,
so caring and serious as to make me well.

STINGO   Incredible, the way he looked after you.
Nathan should have been a doctor.

SOPHIE   Yes, he so very much wanted to be a doctor.

STINGO   So why does this saintly and compassionate man
become the living terror we saw today?

SOPHIE   Oh, Stingo, when Nathan is in one of his bad times,
like today – one of his *tempêtes*, I call them –
he start to scream and call me a Polish pig.
I have to be so *patient* with Nathan then.
I know he is becoming very sick
and that all is not right with him.
I just turn away and keep silent,
waiting for the *tempête* to go away.
Then I know he will be kind and sweet to me again,
so full of *tendresse* and loving.

(Outside, darkness is falling. Sophie and Stingo do not hear the street door in the hallway opening quietly. Nathan creeps shamefacedly back into the house. He slips into Sophie's room and disappears into the shadows. Sophie hands Stingo back his handkerchief.)

Thank you...

(As she does so, Stingo gently takes hold of her wrist.)

STINGO   Sophie, how did you get this number on your arm?

SOPHIE *(almost whispered)*
    Oswiecim...

STINGO   *Where?...*

SOPHIE   Auschwitz...

(There is a moment's silence.)

SOPHIE   You've been kind. Good night...

(Stingo watches as Sophie slowly crosses the hallway to her room and closes the door quietly behind her. As she sits down on the bed Nathan emerges from the shadows.)

SOPHIE   Nathan!... Oh, Nathan!

(Nathan rushes across the room, falls on his knees in front of Sophie, and embraces her desperately.)

NATHAN *(weeping)*
    How could I do it to you?
    How could I hurt you so?...

SOPHIE   There, Nathan... Nathan...

NATHAN   Sophie, I love you so,
    I love you so!

(He buries his head in her lap.)

SOPHIE   Shh... Nathan, darling... Nathan...
    Nathan, my dearest...
    Darling Nathan...

(They embrace passionately.)

(Quick curtain)

ACT II

Scene 1

(The boarding house, the following morning. Sophie and Nathan, obviously in high spirits, run down the stairs. They are both dressed in elegant clothes of the nineteen-thirties period. Nathan knocks on Stingo's door.)

NATHAN *(from behind the door)*
    Stingo! Oh, Stingo!
    Up and at 'em, boy –
    we're going to Coney Island!

STINGO   Leave me alone!

NATHAN *(putting his head round the door)*
    Come on, Cracker, let's hit the road!
    (with exaggerated Southern accent)
    We gonna hab ol' Pompey hitch up the coach-an'-foah
    an' hab us a little picnic outin' down by the seashoah!

(Stingo tries to block the door, but Nathan has his foot in it.)

STINGO   Get out of here!

NATHAN   Stingo, *Stingo* – take it easy.
    No offence meant, kid.

STINGO   Get your goddamned foot out of the door
    and leave me alone!

NATHAN   Aw, come on, open up.
    I'm really sorry about yesterday.
    Let's make up and be pals.

STINGO   I don't want to be pals.
    I don't have to take your rotten insults –
    and *don't* call me Cracker!

NATHAN   All right, Stingo.
    I won't use the word again.
    Forgive me, will you?

STINGO   Scram – I want to be alone.

SOPHIE *(from behind the door)*
    Please, Stingo.
    Nathan didn't mean to hurt your feelings.
    We just want to be friends
    and take you out on this beautiful day.
    Please come with us!

(Hearing Sophie's voice, Stingo relaxes somewhat. Nathan takes his foot out of the door.)

STINGO   Well, okay – but *he* owes me an apology.

NATHAN   I'm sorry, Stingo.
    I apologise. Let's forget it, okay?
    But we're serious about our little outing.
    Why don't you come over to Sophie's room
    and have some coffee with us?
    Then off we'll go to Coney Island!

SOPHIE   Stingo, *do* come with us!

STINGO *(after a pause)*
                All right, I'll come. *(lamely)* Thanks…

(Sophie and Nathan run excitedly into Sophie's room. Stingo, with sudden enthusiasm at the prospect of the outing, dons a colourful tie and smart summer jacket. Coming quickly out of his room he meets Yetta in the hallway.)

YETTA   Good morning, young man!

STINGO   Good morning, Mrs. Zimmerman…

(In Sophie's room, Nathan puts a record of tango music on the phonograph. The music wafts through the half-open door into the hallway.)

YETTA *(inspecting Stingo admiringly)*
                Well, *well*! Wherefore art *thou* going, Romeo?
                I'll bet some lucky girl's
                gonna have her dream come true today!
(She chuckles and gives him a confidential nudge.)
                Well, I do like to see my tenants enjoy life!
                You know, I call this place Yetta's Liberty Hall.
                Not that I don't gotta have rules, mind you.
                But what I mean is, this place is for grown-ups!

STINGO *(awkwardly)*
                Right, Mrs. Zimmerman…

YETTA   I'm running no brothel, you understand.
                But once in a while, you wanta have a girl in your room –
                (with an expansive gesture)
                – you *have* a girl in your room!
                That's right, I like to see people enjoy life…

(Yetta disappears into the back of the house. Stingo knocks on Sophie's door.)

SOPHIE and NATHAN
                Entrez!

(Stingo goes into the room, which is filled with the sound of the tango record playing. At first, Sophie and Nathan are nowhere in sight. Then they suddenly appear from behind a screen on the far side of the room, dancing stylishly. Stingo, though taken aback, is delighted by their little show.)

NATHAN *(while dancing)*
                A hobby of ours…
                Today we're wearing early thirties.
                We also do twenties, World War One period –
                even Gay Nineties.

STINGO   Don't people stare?

NATHAN   Sure they stare –

SOPHIE   – that's part of the fun!

NATHAN   Dressed like this we have individuality – style.

(With a final flourish, Sophie and Nathan finish their dance. Nathan takes the needle off the record.)

NATHAN   Those people out there on the street,
                they're all drab, all alike.
                Walking around in uniform.

(He sits down near Stingo. Sophie prepares coffee in the kitchen area.)
        (nodding towards Sophie)
        Look at her, isn't she something?
        Hey, dollbaby, come over here!

SOPHIE   I'm busy, can't you see?

NATHAN   Hey, come over here!
        (winking at Stingo)
        Can't keep my hands off her...
(Sophie walks over and plops down in Nathan's lap.)
        Give me a kiss.

SOPHIE   One kiss, that's all.
        (kissing him quickly on the cheek)
        There – that's all you deserve.

NATHAN   I can't keep my ha-a-a-nds off *(falsetto)* you-u-u.

SOPHIE *(giggling)*
        Enough! No more kisses.

(She jumps off his lap.)

NATHAN   You're a cheater, a tease!
        Worse than any little *yenta* from Brooklyn!
        (another sly wink to Stingo)
        What do you think of that, Stingo?
        Here I am, a good Jewish boy pushing thirty years old;
        I fall crazy in love with a Polish *shiksa*
        and she keeps her sweet treasure all locked up?

STINGO   Bad news – a form of sadism.

NATHAN   When I first met this one here
        she was a rag and bone and a hank of hair.

SOPHIE *(serving the coffee)*
        I looked like an old witch, a real wreck.

NATHAN   Massive doses of iron did the trick.
        Soon she began to bloom like a rose.
        (running his hand through her hair)
        God, you're something...
        Such a very *beautiful* something...

SOPHIE *(tenderly)*
        Thank you for making me to bloom like a rose.

NATHAN   Not *to* bloom, just bloom.

SOPHIE   Stinking infinitive!
        Such a language – too many words!
        Just the words for *vélocité*:
        'fast', 'rapid', 'quick' – all the same thing!

STINGO   Also 'swift' –
NATHAN   – 'speedy' –
STINGO   – 'hasty' –
NATHAN   – 'fleet' –
STINGO   – 'snappy'!

SOPHIE *(laughing)*
        Stop! Too much, this English!

NATHAN *(to Stingo)*
>What brought you to Brooklyn?

STINGO   I came to New York to become a writer.

NATHAN   You're a writer?
>I once wanted to write myself.
>At Harvard I wrote a lot of poetry
>and some lousy short stories.
>In the end I had the sense to realise
>my true gifts were in science...
>I turned my piercing mind...
>... toward the seething arcana...
>... of human... protoplasm...

(During the latter part of the preceding Nathan's delivery, though ironic, has become more and more inward, as though talking to himself. Now he suddenly looks at Stingo very intently.)

>But you, you're from the South.
>That makes you a *southern* writer, doesn't it?

STINGO *(uneasily)*
>Well, I guess so...

NATHAN *(quietly, with emphasis)*
>You know, you *Confederate* types –
>*(lapsing again into a lazy drawl)*
>Y-*all* in'erest me *ve-e-ry* much.

STINGO *(nervously, taking up the southern accent)*
>Why, Nathan ole hoss,
>you Brooklyn folks *in'erest* us boys down home, too.

NATHAN   Hardly a joking matter, kid.
>What about all those lynchings?
>Worthy of nothing more
>than your attempt at humour?

STINGO *(with mounting irritation)*
>It wasn't me who started that cotton-picking accent!

SOPHIE   Please, Nathan! No more about lynchings.
>*(to Stingo)*
>All week he's been talking about lynchings;
>I can't get him to stop.
(She turns back to Nathan.)
>Please, darling, we were having such a lovely time!

NATHAN *(persistently, disregarding Sophie)*
>As I was saying – what about those lynchings, kid?

STINGO *(exasperated)*
>Well, what *about* them, for Christ's sake?

NATHAN *(pointing accusingly at Stingo)*
>I'll tell you what –
>I say the fate of those black victims in the South
>is as barbaric as any act performed by the Nazis
>under Adolph Hitler. You agree?

STINGO Of course I agree – it's horrible! They're *both* horrible!
    But that doesn't make *all* Southerners into lynchers –
    Goddammit, I'm not going to swallow that line!
    And what gives you the right to pass judgement?
    You've never even been near the South.

NATHAN As a Jew, I regard myself as an authority
    on anguish and suffering –

SOPHIE *(quickly stepping between the two of them and facing Nathan)*
    Stop this talk *right now*!
    And stop shouting at Stingo!
    Stingo had nothing to do with any lynchings.
    Stingo's *sweet*.
    And *you're* sweet, Nathan Landau.
    Vraiment, je t'adore, chéri.

(Nathan cannot help submitting to Sophie's sheer charm and brio. His self-righteous anger disappears as quickly as it arose. He laughs softly.)

NATHAN Stingo, old pal, I'm just an ass!
    Really I am – an *ass*!
    (holding out his hand)
    I'm sorry.
    I know it's not *all* bad down there.
    I'll make you a promise –
    never to jump on you about the South again.
    Okay?
    Sophie, you're a witness!

(Stingo takes Nathan's proffered hand.)

SOPHIE Good! I'll see you keep your word!

NATHAN *(to Stingo)*
    You know, I think we're going to become great friends!

SOPHIE We're *all* going to be great friends!

NATHAN Off we go! To the beach!

SOPHIE To the beach!

(They go off happily together.)

Interlude

(The Narrator appears…)

NARRATOR Coney Island!
    Golden effervescent air!
    A popcorn, candy apple and sauerkraut fragrance!
    That day, we took all the wild rides.
    Sophie reached a realm past simple joy,
    crying out in ecstasy.
    Never have I seen such glee,
    such visceral bliss, such rich terror!

Scene 2

(The scene presents two locations: Stingo's room in the boarding house in Brooklyn, summer 1947, and Professor Bieganski's study in Cracow, December 1938.)

NARRATOR   And so indeed we became the best of friends.
Nathan took on the role
of brother, mentor, constructive critic.

Brooklyn...

(Stingo and Nathan are deep in conversation.)

NATHAN   I admire your courage, kid.

STINGO   Why?

NATHAN   I really admire what you're doing,
setting out to write something else about the South.

STINGO   What's so courageous about writing of the South?
It's the place I know best.

NATHAN   It's simply that you're at the end of a tradition;
Southern writing as a force
will be over within a few years.
Another genre will take its place.

STINGO *(amused)*
Nathan, you're an expert on *cells*.
What the hell do you know
about literary genres and traditions?

NATHAN   You forget – I was planning to write myself.

(Nathan and Stingo continue their conversation.)

NARRATOR   Sophie also continued to confide in me,
trusting me with further revelations.
Moreover, she confessed to being not quite truthful
in her recital of past events.
There was, for example, the question of her adored father,
the eminent Professor Bieganski.
Was he really the model of paternal rectitude and decency,
the brave libertarian, the socialist paterfamilias
that Sophie had so artfully created?
Hardly...

Cracow...

(Bieganski is dictating to Sophie, who is taking shorthand.)

BIEGANSKI   ... After a period when government policy towards the Jewish question
has been one of weakness and compromise – in reality a betrayal of the
fundamental interests of the Polish people – we must ask ourselves: what
is the right direction for Poland now? How are we to deal with a large
population of superfluous Jews?...

(He continues the dictation.)

NARRATOR   At first Sophie was only vaguely aware
            of her father's political beliefs.
            But when, as submissive and dutiful daughter
            she was obliged to become his secretary,
            she began to divine the depth and extent
            of his fiery enthusiasms.

BIEGANSKI   Previously I advocated a policy of rigorous segregation, such as my
            proposal for separate 'ghetto benches' in our universities. However, such
            measures have the defect of leaving the problem in place; I now view
            them as temporary, a mere stop-gap. A more permanent solution is
            called for; some form of expatriation perhaps, large-scale population
            transfers...

(Bieganski continues his dictation to Sophie.)

Brooklyn...

NATHAN   Of course, my artistic hopes were the result
            of a typically ambitious Jewish mother.
            I can see now all I had going for me was that I was Jewish.

STINGO   How do you mean?

NATHAN   I'm quite certain that Jewish writing
            will be the next important force in American literature.

STINGO *(on the defensive)*
            Oh, will it?

NATHAN   I didn't say it would be the *only* force,
            just the *important* one.

STINGO   Well, at least you haven't told me the novel is dead...

(The conversation continues.)

NARRATOR   And now Sophie had drawn upon her
            the whole culminating design
            of her father's hate-drenched philosophy...

Cracow...

BIEGANSKI *(dictating)*
            The continuing economic crisis makes the matter urgent. Can we really
            permit alien ghetto Jews to take jobs from the thousands of honest Poles
            flooding into our cities? Our nation can no longer delay. A solution must
            be imposed: total abolishment of the Jewish element in Poland.
(Bieganski is struck by a thought.)
            One moment – that could be expressed more forcefully... *(ponders)*
            Ah, I have it. Change 'total abolishment' to 'extermination'. Yes, that's it:
            'Extermination of the Jewish element...' Excellent...Type out those last
            few pages immediately, please.

(Horrified by what she has heard, Sophie leaves the room.)

Brooklyn...

NATHAN   As a child, I was supposed to become
            a great fiddle player, another Heifetz or Menuhin.
            But I lacked the touch, music wasn't my *métier*.

STINGO	But as compensation you have the phonograph and all those records.
NATHAN	Yes, thanks to Sophie; she really taught me to care about music, as she has taught me so many things. You're welcome to come up any time and play the records.
STINGO	Thanks, Nathan...
NATHAN	But treat them with care, they're fragile.
STINGO	I will.
NATHAN	You know, I predict that soon there'll be an unbreakable record, with an entire symphony on one side.

(The conversation continues.)

Cracow...

(Sophie comes slowly back into Bieganski's study with the typescript of the pamphlet.)

BIEGANSKI	Ah, you've completed it?
SOPHIE	Yes, Papa...
BIEGANSKI	Good. *(taking the typescript from Sophie)* What's the matter Sophie? You look quite pale. Would you like a cup of tea?
SOPHIE	No, thank you, Papa.

BIEGANSKI *(putting his arm around her shoulder)*
    Come, my dear.
    You must have some tea.
    You look pale and cold.

SOPHIE *(recoiling)*
    No, thank you, Papa,
    I really don't want any tea.

BIEGANSKI	Very well, as you wish...

(Bieganski begins to read the pamphlet.)

Brooklyn...

NATHAN	How's the novel going?
STINGO	Slowly.
NATHAN	Can I see the work in progress?
STINGO	It's at an early stage...
NATHAN	Oh, come on – why not? We're friends. I won't interfere. I won't comment, I won't even make suggestions. I'd just love to see it.

(Stingo succumbs and hands over the manuscript.)

STINGO   All right... Here's the the first part...

NATHAN   Can't wait to read it. Thanks...

(Nathan leaves.)

Cracow...

(Bieganski is checking through the pamphlet with increasing irritation.)

BIEGANSKI   Who is this Neville Chamberlain
who so loves the works of Richard Wagner?

SOPHIE   What do you mean, Papa?

BIEGANSKI   It should be *Houston* Chamberlain –
you've confused the two names every time,
you stupid girl!
This means all the footnotes
as well as the text are incorrect.

SOPHIE   I'm sorry, Papa...

BIEGANSKI *(furious)*
I don't know where you got your body,
but you did not get your brains from me.
Your intelligence is *pulp*, just like your mother's!
(shouting)
Pulp! D'you hear?

(Sophie rushes from the room weeping. The scene dims quickly.)

Scene 3

(Sophie and Stingo are in Sophie's room in the boarding house; summer 1947.)

SOPHIE   Extermination!
Oh God, extermination!...
When my father dictate that vile pamphlet,
at first I am so confused and fearful
I don't understand what he say,
it is all so senseless, so cruel.
But then, oh then came the truth:
extermination!
He wanted all the Jewish people killed,
all slaughtered!
He was a murderer, a butcher –
my own father!

And this man, this father,
who gave me breath and flesh,
I see he have no more feeling for me than a servant;
he shout at me and curse me,
he treat me like a slave.

And so I realise I hate my father.
I hate him – *hate* him!
And I hate my husband too, his lackey.
I had no more love for either of them
than stone-faced strangers...

My father's terrible ideas did not save him.
As soon as the Germans arrived in Cracow
he and Casimir were rounded up and shot to death.
But do you know, Stingo?
When this happened I could not be sad,
I have no feeling of loss...

STINGO   Sophie, why did you say you loved your father?

SOPHIE   Forgive me, Stingo.
Before, I have told so many lies about my life,
such an abundance of lies I have told you!
I am the avatar of *menteuses*...

(Suddenly, from the hallway comes the sound of Nathan's boisterous entrance. He bursts into Sophie's room in wild excitement. He is carrying a briefcase and a bottle of champagne.)

NATHAN   Get out the glasses!
We are going to celebrate!

SOPHIE   Celebrate what, darling?

NATHAN   We've had a great breakthrough at the lab!
Remember the experiment I told you about
that had us stumped all last week – the enzyme problem?

SOPHIE   Oh yes...

NATHAN   We crashed through on that this morning!
We got the whole problem beaten – I mean *licked*!

SOPHIE   You have?...

NATHAN   We've been working on this for months,
it's been our toughest challenge by far.
Now we have a clear road
to one of the biggest medical advances in recent years!

SOPHIE   Oh Nathan, I'm so excited for you!

STINGO   Nathan, that's wonderful news...

SOPHIE   Quick – the champagne!

NATHAN   No – wait! There's something *else*.

(With dramatic reverence Nathan kneels down in front of Stingo, removes the novel manuscript from his briefcase, and formally hands it over.)

NATHAN   You've read Faulkner, Penn Warren, Thomas Wolfe –
even Carson McCullers.
And I know I'm breaking my promise about no criticism.
(He jumps up, grasps Stingo by the shoulders, and plants a kiss on his forehead.)
Twenty two years old, and my God, can you write!
Of course you've read those writers,
but you've *absorbed* them, kid,
made them your own.
You've got your own *voice*.
Give me more!

STINGO *(overwhelmed)*
Nathan, do you really mean it?

NATHAN *(opening the champagne)*
>That's the most exciting hundred pages
>by an unknown writer I've ever read!
>That party scene at the club, for example – it's terrific!
>The little scrap of dialogue between mother and maid –
>it just seems right on target.
>And the sense of summer in the South,
>I don't know how you do it!

(Nathan pours the champagne. Sophie hugs Stingo excitedly.)

SOPHIE   Now I know it, Stingo – you *are* a genius!

NATHAN *(raising his glass)*
>I drink to Stingo, the next great American writer!

SOPHIE   To Stingo!

STINGO   Nathan, I drink to your success,
>and to science and all her benefits!

(They all drink a toast.)

NATHAN   You know, maybe we should
>go down South, see what it's like.
>This writing of yours whets my appetite.
>How would that suit you, old buddy –
>a trip through the old Confederacy?

STINGO   Nathan, that would be just tremendous!

SOPHIE   Oh yes, let's go!

NATHAN   Yes, it's *time* I saw the South.
>I'll confess to ignorance.
>How can I hate a place I've never seen or known?

STINGO *(dryly)* Right, Nathan...

NATHAN   I'm with you, kid – we'll make that trip!
>You can be the guide.

SOPHIE   Oh Stingo, I can't wait!

NATHAN   And I give you my word:
>while we're down there I'll put my prejudice on hold.
>Unlike that old bastard Ginsburg I won't be a spoiler.

STINGO   Ginsburg?...

NATHAN   Here, let me tell you...

>Well, at a club banquet Shapiro proposes yet again his perennially
>blackballed friend Tannenbaum for membership. At the other end of the
>table, dozing quietly after a heavy dinner, sits Ginsburg, Shapiro's arch
>enemy, who he hopes will not wake up...

(Nathan begins his comic routine.)
>*(as Shapiro; unctuous, oleaginous)*
>'To tell you what a great human being Max Tannenbaum is I must use
>the entire English alphabet! From A to Z I will tell you about this
>beautiful man!'

(Nathan surveys the imaginary banquet table.)

(silky, sly)
'A he is Admirable.
B he is Beneficial.
C he is Charming.
D he is Delightful.
E he is Educated.
F he is Friendly.
G he is Good-hearted.
H he is a Helluva nice guy.
I he is Inna-resting' –
Suddenly, Ginsburg wakes up
and leaps to his feet:
(as Ginsburg; thundering)
'J joost a minute!' *(a majestic pause)*
(stabbing the air with his finger)
'K he's a Kike!
L he's a Lummox!
M he's a Moron!
N he's a Nayfish!
O he's an Ox!
P he's a Prick!
Q he's a Queer!
R he's a Red!
S he's a Schlemiel!
T he's a Tochis!
U you can have him!
V ve don't vant him!
W X Y Z – I blackball the shmuck!'
(mutual hilarity)

(Quick curtain)

ACT III

Prologue

(The Narrator appears...)

NARRATOR   Yes, Nathan was utterly, fatally glamorous.
How could I have failed
to have the most helpless crush
on such a generous, life-giving friend.
I became quite simply devoted to him.
My delight in him was only surpassed by Sophie,
whose unflagging passion for Nathan struck me with awe.
I yearned for her passionately,
yet yielded her up willingly to my friend.

Happy though I was,
it was impossible not to remain haunted
by what Sophie told me of her past.
One rainy afternoon in August
she told me of her time in Warsaw,
when she came to know Wanda...

Scene 1

(Warsaw, March 1943. An apartment room, sparsely furnished and illuminated by a single lamp. The window blinds are drawn. Sophie and Wanda are having an agitated conversation. Sophie's children, Jan and Eva, are playing quietly in the room.)

WANDA   Sophie, I'm appealing to you to help the Movement.

SOPHIE   No – I've already told you I cannot help you.

WANDA   But Sophie, we desperately need
those captured documents translated.
They're worth their weight in gold to us.
With a translation we can find out
so much about their plans;
it would be such a help to the Resistance – to us all!
You speak perfect German, and can do it.

SOPHIE   No, Wanda, I can't do it!
I dare not risk it, I have to think of my children.

WANDA   I'm asking you to help save *all* our children!
Those documents concern the Nazis' attack on our children
with their monstrous Lebensborn programme!
How can you refuse to do this when you know
they've already kidnapped hundreds of children
and sent them away into captivity?
Their families will never see them again!

SOPHIE   I know, I know...
Our neighbour Katarina just lost her little boy...

WANDA   It might be your own children next!
Just imagine it – Jan or Eva snatched from your arms in the street
and shipped off to the glorious Reich!
They would disappear from your life for ever!

SOPHIE   Oh please Wanda, stop! I can't bear it!

WANDA *(relentlessly)*
    You know as well as I do that once there,
    they'd be placed in homes faithful to the Führer,
    renamed Karl, Trudi or Heinrich and raised as perfect little Nazis!
    Don't you want to help fight this?

SOPHIE
    Yes, of course I do!
    But surely you understand that by helping you
    I put my children in even greater danger?

WANDA
    Other women in the Resistance have children.

SOPHIE
    I'm not '*other women*', and I'm not in the Resistance!
    I'm *myself*! It's easy for you to talk like this,
    you don't have any children.

    You tell me I should help you, but how can I?
    Do not think badly of me, Wanda,
    but I dare not take the risk.
    We are all trapped in this inferno,
    living in fear and dread with no means of escape.
    Every day we face such danger;
    I have endured months of terror,
    waiting for a raid, a knock on the door.
    Oh, how can you know, as I do,
    a mother's worst fears:
    that you might lose your children,
    taken away, destroyed?

    You must know how I hate these evil demons
    who have overrun our country.
    I am not neutral, but I cannot join you in the struggle;
    my first duty is to *my* children, Jan and Eva.
    For if I were to disappear who would there be to protect them?
    How would they survive this terrible war?
    They have no father, no family – all gone.
    I am all they have left.
    Please Wanda, don't ask for more than I can give…

WANDA
    Look, translating documents puts you at no great risk.
    We can deliver them to you here quite safely;
    no-one would suspect.
    And there are so many other things you could do
    that would be invaluable:
    monitoring radio broadcasts, collecting information.
    Frankly, I find it offensive you seem unable to sacrifice –

SOPHIE
    I've *sacrificed*!
    I've lost a husband and a father already
    and my mother is dying of tuberculosis!
    How much *do* I have to sacrifice, in the name of God?

WANDA
    You must reconsider, Sophie!

SOPHIE
    No, no, Wanda, please, please, *please*!

WANDA
    You can longer treat us this way!

SOPHIE
    It's no use – I can't, I can't!

WANDA
    You have to assume responsibility,
    have to make a choice!

SOPHIE | I am a mother and I must listen to my conscience –
it won't let me do this!

WANDA | Sophie, I'm appealing to you as a Pole.
Consider what you can do for all of us!

SOPHIE | I've told you and I'll tell you again:
I can't, I won't!

WANDA | Consider your country, consider Poland!

SOPHIE | I've already made my choice!

WANDA | I'm appealing to your sense of decency as a human being.
Sophie, I'm appealing to you in the name of humanity!

SOPHIE | No! I will not get involved.
I mean it, that's final!

Interlude

NARRATOR | But Wanda's brave defiance came to nought;
she was soon netted in a Gestapo round-up.
Sophie was also arrested, for smuggling food into the city.
Shortly afterwards, both found themselves
on the same train to Auschwitz…

Scene 2

(Poland, March 1943. An ancient rail car, dilapidated and dirty. Though all the windows are boarded up we aware of the movement of the train. The carriage is packed with people, bunched up together on the tattered seats, standing, lying on the floor. In the corner seat an old woman, crazed with fear, sits weeping and clutching some few last possessions. Propped up against one of the seats an intense young man scribbles furiously in a notebook in the dim light. Sophie is sitting protectively clasping her two children on either side.)

PRISONERS *(a collective sigh of weariness and misery)*
Ah!…

(Wanda is seen struggling through the mass of people, stepping over reclining bodies. She has an ugly bruise on the cheek. She sees Sophie and the children.)

WANDA | Sophie! What in God's name are *you* doing here?

SOPHIE | Wanda! Oh, God in heaven – they got you too!

(Hardly able to believe she is confronted by Wanda, Sophie puts one of the children on her lap to make room on the seat beside her.)

PRISONERS | Ah!…

WANDA | They arrested everyone in our building – a clean sweep of it.
Oh God, they picked up so many people in the Movement.
It's a catastrophe!

SOPHIE *(seeing the bruise on Wanda's face)*
What did they do to you, Wanda darling?

WANDA | Some Gestapo ape threw me down the stairs,
then stamped on me. Oh, these…
(She raises her eyes upward.)
It's not so bad.
Nothing is broken, I think.

OLD WOMAN (*wailing*)
>They can't arrest me, they can't!...
>I have immunity...

YOUNG MAN For pity's sake hold your noise!

WANDA Poor Sophie. Imagine *you* falling into their filthy trap.

SOPHIE I was caught bringing some meat for poor Mama.
>At least they allowed me to keep the children.

WANDA Sophie, where we're going
>the children will be no safer than we are.
>Your best hope will be to try and get them sent away.

SOPHIE (*breaking down*)
>Sent away? Oh, my God!...

OLD WOMAN I have immunity, I tell you.
>I'm a niece of Wieniawski...

YOUNG MAN Who the hell cares?

OLD WOMAN Surely they'll understand that, won't they, these Germans?
>After all, they like music...
>Here, look, I have one of his manuscripts –

YOUNG MAN The Germans will light a fire with your stupid manuscript!

(*The old woman dissolves in wailing tears.*)

PRISONERS Ah!...

WANDA (*to Sophie*)
>Come on now, keep your courage up.
>You never know what might happen,
>what piece of luck come your way.
>After all, you're young, an attractive woman.
>If you get the opportunity with one of those pigs, use it.
>Men are all the same...
>Sleeping with them won't be collaboration,
>it'll be espionage – a fifth column!

SOPHIE Oh, but Wanda, I *can't* have the children sent away –
>it's more than I could bear!

WANDA My poor Sophie, do you think you'll have a choice?
>In this war we all suffer:
>Jews, Poles, Czechs, Russians, gypsies – and the children.
>It doesn't matter if you're five years old or fifty –
(*She is struck by an idea.*)
>Wait – I've thought of something...
>Yes – of course! You must get them
>into that Lebensborn programme!
>Then at least you *know* they'll survive!

SOPHIE (*horrified*)
>You speak of survival?...
>Oh, my God!...

WANDA Listen, they have a chance of being accepted;
>they already speak the language
>and could easily pass as German kids.
(*Sophie weeps hopelessly.*)

Go ahead and cry, darling.
The idea sounds bizarre, I know.
But at least we know
this unspeakable Lebensborn thing really exists.
It's awful, but it could be their best hope.
Who knows? – you might even be able
to keep track of them.
After all, this damnable war can't go on for ever...

PRISONERS   Ah!...

(The stage gradually darkens...)

Interlude

(The Narrator appears. The quiet singing of the prisoners continues to be heard in the background.)

NARRATOR   But it was not to be.

PRISONERS   Ah!...

NARRATOR   On arrival, most of those on the train perished immediately.
Among them was Eva Maria Zawistowska, aged eight years...
Wanda, Jan, and Sophie herself fell into
'the slow hands of the living damnation'.
That great spirit Wanda didn't last long,
tortured by bestial guards and strung up on a wire.
Sophie herself was luckier;
her skills as linguist and stenographer were needed.
She went to work for the camp commandant,
Obersturmbannführer Rudolph Höss.
So it was she became both victim and accomplice...

Scene 3

(Auschwitz concentration camp, October 1943. An attic room in the camp Commandant's house. The room has been set up as an office and contains a plain pinewood table with a telephone and some papers on it, a filing cabinet, a few chairs, and a couch against one wall. In an area invisible from the main part of the room, a small desk with typewriter, a sink, and a medicine cabinet on the wall. Sophie, dressed in a drab smock and a headscarf covering her shaven head, is taking dictation from the camp Commandant, Rudolph Höss.)

HÖSS *(dictating)*
'...whereas it is respectfully suggested that in the specific matter of the Greek Jews' – I'm not going too fast, am I?

SOPHIE   *Nein, mein Kommandant.*

HÖSS *(continuing dictation)*
' – alternative destinations in the occupied territories of the East, such as KL Treblinka or KL Sobibór, be considered.' End paragraph '*Heil Hitler!*' Sign as usual and type.
(picking up another letter from the table and scanning it with irritation)
Polish – impossible language!
They know they're supposed to communicate in German.
(handing the letter to Sophie)
Here – what does it say?

SOPHIE *(translating)*
> 'Honoured Commandant... It is with great regret that I must most respectfully inform you of the impossibility of providing the quantity of gravel ordered by your command on the scheduled delivery date. Begging your indulgence, honoured Commandant, but the extremely soggy condition of the ground around the quarry' –

HÖSS *(exasperated)*
> Enough! Damn them to hell, these Polish half-wits!
> Send a translation with the following note
> to Hauptsturmführer Weitzmann –
> 'Weitzmann: build a fire under this piddler and get him moving!'
> *(working himself up into a fury of resentment)*
> This means further delay in the building programme –
> and more trouble from Berlin.
> Those damned bureaucrats at headquarters!
> They're totally unreasonable;
> they ask the superhuman from a mere human
> who has done the very best he can.
> They've never had to deal with these idiot Poles!
> *What have I done wrong?*
> I've done my faithful best and this is the thanks I get –
> kicked upstairs to Oranienburg under the pretence it's a promotion.
> This whole thing – it's sickening.
> I know how well I've performed my duty,
> but they've never shown the slightest bit of gratitude –

(Höss is suddenly attacked by a violent migraine. He sways on his feet, then staggers toward the couch.)

HÖSS *(groaning)*
> Aaargh!...
> For God's sake, where are my pills?
> Quick... my pills!

(He collapses in agony on the couch. Sophie retrieves the pills from the medicine cabinet, fills a glass of water from the tap and hurries over to Höss, who gulps them down.)

SOPHIE   Shall I call the doctor?

HÖSS   No. Just be quiet.
> I can't bear anything at the moment.

(Sophie goes back to the sink and dampens a towel. She returns to Höss, loosens the collar of his uniform jacket, and carefully mops his brow. Höss begins to relax.)

HÖSS   It's better.

SOPHIE   I'm glad, *mein Kommandant*.

(Sophie stands waiting uncertainly. Höss looks her up and down.)

HÖSS   You may sit down.

(Sophie seats herself on a chair by the couch.)

HÖSS   How did you come here?

SOPHIE *(very nervously at first, but gradually gaining confidence)*
> Fate, I think...

HÖSS   What do you mean, fate?

SOPHIE	Fate brought me to you. I think I knew only *you* would understand.
HÖSS	Understand what?
SOPHIE	You would understand a mistake has been made, *mein Kommandant*. I hope you will believe me when I say my imprisonment here is a terrible miscarriage of justice. I am guilty of nothing truly serious, and should be set free. When you consider my personal background and knowledge –
HÖSS	Knowledge – what knowledge?

(Sophie pulls out some folded newsprint from the side of her shoe and hands it over to Höss.)

| SOPHIE | I took a chance, *mein Kommandant*,
I kept this against the rules.
But I want you to know this pamphlet
represents everything I stand for. |

HÖSS *(reading)*
　　　　　　'Poland's Jewish Question' by Zbigniew Bieganski,
　　　　　　Professor of Jurisprudence, University of Cracow...

(Höss impassively scans through the pamphlet.)

SOPHIE *(trembling)*
　　　　　　It is one of the earliest Polish documents
　　　　　　detailing a 'final solution' to the Jewish problem.
　　　　　　I collaborated with my father in writing it...

HÖSS *(looking up)*
　　　　　　What's the matter? You're white.

SOPHIE	Nothing, *mein Kommandant*. I'm just a bit faint. It will go away.
HÖSS	You maintain, then, that in the matter of your internment here you are innocent?
SOPHIE	I freely admit my guilt on the minor charge which caused me to be sent here: smuggling food. I was trying to help my mother who was very sick. I only ask this misdemeanor be weighed against my record as a Polish sympathiser with National Socialism, and I implore you to reconsider my imprisonment.

(Höss tosses the pamphlet on the floor.)

| HÖSS | This document means nothing to me.
It proves very little, only that you despise Jews.
That does not impress me very much,
it is a widespread sentiment. |

(In despair, Sophie is on the point of bursting into tears. She tries desperately to control herself. Höss regards her with renewed interest.)

<blockquote>

You have been flirting shamelessly with me...
(caressing Sophie's cheek)
You are a very beautiful young woman:
your fair complexion, the shape of your face –
as fine a face as I've ever seen.

In certain women
there is a pure and radiant beauty –
fair of hair, fair of skin –
that inspires me to idolise that beauty,
and desire it to the point of worship...

</blockquote>

(Höss suddenly lunges forward, grabs Sophie by the waist, and feverishly covers her face and neck in clumsy kisses. At this moment there is a knock at the door. Höss curses quietly and hastily composes himself, buttoning up his tunic and smoothing back his dishevelled hair. He motions Sophie to the desk.)

<blockquote>

Yes? Who is it?

</blockquote>

(The door opens and the camp Doctor enters the room.)

DOCTOR   You wished to see me?

HÖSS   Yes. I am having endless trouble from Berlin
over production statistics in the mines.
We *have* to increase the labour force.

DOCTOR   You already know my opinion on that matter.
Only really strong and healthy prisoners
should be selected for that type of employment;
sick ones become an expensive drain on medical facilities.
But I'm aware the views of a mere doctor count for little –

HÖSS *(interrupting with irritation)*
You know well I am answerable to a higher authority
which is now insisting on one thing – increased production
at all mines and armament plants in this command.
Even an aged and sick person is capable of
a certain number of thermal units of energy.
I might suggest you not appear so... so... *concerned.*
It could harm your career.

DOCTOR   I was obliged to leave my career when drafted.
Nowadays I try to forget it.

HÖSS   With a little help from the brandy bottle, it seems...

DOCTOR   It has become a necessity to me
in fulfilling my duties here;
duties which consist mainly
of deciding who lives, who dies –
even including the children.

(Hearing this, Sophie reacts with terror.)

HÖSS   Come, we must face the facts.
I have to put these prisoners to work.

DOCTOR   I suppose we could see what use might be made
of those prisoners at present submitted to...

(His voice trails off.)

HÖSS   'Special action'?…

(The Doctor looks steadily at Höss for a moment.)

DOCTOR   Very well. I'll look into it.

(He quietly leaves the room. Höss approaches Sophie very closely. She tries to hide her fear and loathing.)

HÖSS   I would risk a great deal to have relations with you.
              If I were not leaving here, I would take the risk.
              But they have got rid of me, and I must go.
              You must go too.
              Tomorrow I'm sending you back
              to Block Two where you came from.

SOPHIE   *Herr Kommandant,*
              I know I can't ask much for myself,
              but I beg you to do one thing for me
              before you send me back.
              I have a young son in the camp.
              His name is Jan Zawistowski; he's ten years old.
              I beg you to consider some way he might be released.

HÖSS *(angered)*
              But that's against regulations!
              It's out of the question for me to do that!

(Sophie falls on her knees in front of Höss. He is deeply embarrassed.)

SOPHIE *(becoming hysterical)*
              But *mein Kommandant*, there is a lawful way!
              You could have my child
              moved away from the Children's camp
              and into the Lebensborn programme.
              Send him to the Reich,
              where he would become a good German.
              He is blond and speaks your language perfectly.
              Don't you see how my little boy Jan
              would be excellent for Lebensborn?

(In her desperation Sophie clutches Höss around the knees.)

HÖSS   Get to your feet!
              Demonstrations like this offend me. Get up!
(Sophie slowly rises.)
              (with softer voice)
              I think what you say might be a possible solution.
              I will look into the matter.

SOPHIE *(hardly daring to ask)*
              Please, *mein Kommandant*…
              Give me a definite answer.
              I cannot bear any more uncertainty…

HÖSS   Very well. I will see that he's removed from the camp.

SOPHIE   Forgive me, how can I be sure of this?

HÖSS You have my assurance and word as a German officer.
My word of honour.
(Sophie is speechless with joy.)
You may go now.

SOPHIE *Danke, mein Kommandant.*
Danke...

(Sophie leaves. The scene fades.)

Scene 4

(The Maple Court Lounge, Brooklyn; early autumn 1947. It is early evening. The bar is quiet, sparsely populated with a few customers. Sophie and Stingo are at a table together. They are both smartly dressed, ready for an evening out. There is a bottle of wine and a spare glass on the table.)

SOPHIE I have often wondered, Stingo:
is it best to know of a child's death,
even a terrible one,
or to know the child lives
but you will never see him again?

Höss did not keep his word.
I never got any kind of message from him, ever.
His 'word of honour', indeed!
What a filthy liar!

I never knew what happened to Jan,
whether he die there in Auschwitz
or stayed alive in Germany somewhere.
I never saw my little boy again...

Stingo, I think I've learned to cry again.
Perhaps that means I'm a human being once more.
Only a part of a human being;
but still, a human being...

(Stingo takes hold of her hand. After a pause, Sophie looks at her watch.)

SOPHIE Where is Nathan, I wonder?

STINGO He'll be here soon.

SOPHIE He telephoned me this morning, so *excited.*
He said his research team have make
the *final breakthrough* they were hoping for.
He said it could win the *Nobel Prize!*
Isn't it incredible? Isn't it *formidable?*

(At this moment Nathan approaches the table. His eyes have a dangerous glitter. Sophie rises to greet him.)

SOPHIE Nathan, darling!...

NATHAN *(brushing her off)*
Haven't I told you the only single thing
I absolutely demand from you is *fidelity?*

SOPHIE Nathan, I –

NATHAN And didn't I tell you that if you ever were seen again
with that horse doctor you work for I'd kill you?

SOPHIE   But, Nathan –

NATHAN *(his voice rising)*
                  So, this afternoon he brings you home in his car,
                  you take him up to your room,
                  and you're up there with him for an hour!
                  What did he do – lay you a couple of times?

STINGO   Nathan, take it easy...

SOPHIE   Darling, let me explain!

NATHAN   There's nothing to explain!
                  You'd have kept it secret too,
                  if old Yetta hadn't seen you take him upstairs!

SOPHIE   But Nathan, he's an expert with phonographs.
                  He came to fix ours –

NATHAN   I bet he's an expert, alright!
                  Does he do a quick routine on your vertebrae
                  with those slippery hands of his while he's humping you?
                  The cheap fraud –

STINGO   Hey, Nathan! Calm down, will you?

SOPHIE   No, no, darling, it just isn't true!

NATHAN   Oh, you're some dish, you are,
                  you really are some Polish dumpling!
                  Why did I ever let you degrade yourself
                  working for that charlatan?

SOPHIE   Please, Nathan –

NATHAN   Shut your yap!
                  I've had just about enough of you
                  and your whorish behaviour.

(Sophie covers her ears against the tirade.)

BARMAN   Hey, mister – keep your voice down please!

(Nathan half bows in a deprecatory manner to the barman, then pours himself a glass of wine. Stingo tries desperately to retrieve the situation.)

STINGO   Nathan, let's cut all this ugly talk.
                  We want to propose a toast to *your success*,
                  to *your* great discovery!

NATHAN *(glaring at Stingo)*
                  There will be no toast this evening
                  to victorious Hygeia, but only in honour
                  of my complete dissociation from you two creeps.
(He tips his glass to Sophie.)
                  Dissociation from *you*,
                  the *première putain* of Flatbush Avenue.
                  (to Stingo)
                  And from you, the Dreary Dregs of Dixie.

STINGO *(setting his glass down with a sigh)*
                  Well, to hell with it, then.

NATHAN *(witheringly)*
>Trouble is, old Stingo, turns out you're badly infected
>by the moral degeneracy of the South.

STINGO
>What do you mean?

NATHAN
>That pathetic novel of yours,
>it's nothing more than a passive vessel
>for the usual poisonous racism of those parts.

STINGO
>But I thought you liked it —

NATHAN
>Oh, you've a pretty snappy talent in the Southern mode.
>But you also have all the old clichés.
>Half the characters are nothing more than *caricatures*.
>You may be writing the first Southern comic book.

SOPHIE
>Please, Nathan! Don't talk like that to Stingo.
>He's our friend —

(Nathan turns savagely on Sophie.)

NATHAN
>Tell me, oh beauteous Zawistowska,
>why is it that you inhabit the land of the living?

SOPHIE
>Nathan, what are you saying?

(Nathan becomes increasingly aggressive towards Sophie. Stingo tries to restrain him.)

NATHAN
>Perhaps after all these months
>you can explain the mystery of why you're here,
>walking these streets,
>drenched in enticing perfumery,
>engaged in surreptitious venery —
>in short, making hay while the sun shines?

STINGO
>Nathan, that's enough!
>Enough of all this crazy talk.
>Stop it right now!

(The Barman comes over and tries to quell the mounting furore.)

BARMAN
>Hey Mister — not so loud, please!

SOPHIE
>Oh Nathan, you're so mistaken!
>You know I love you so…

STINGO
>Why do you need to treat her like this?
>Why cause her all this misery?

BARMAN
>Let's have some quiet around here!
>No more of this racket, if you don't mind!
>Take your quarrel somewhere else!

BAR PATRONS
>What's with this guy?
>— What's that he's saying?
>— He is so mad at her!

(Nathan takes hold of Sophie's wrist in an iron grip.)

NATHAN
>What kind of fine subterfuge did you use
>in order that *your* skin might be saved?
>What splendid little tricks and stratagems

sprang from that lovely head of yours
so you might breathe the clear Polish air,
while the multitudes went up in smoke?

SOPHIE I cannot bear to hear this,
I cannot bear it any longer!
No darling, it just isn't true!

BARMAN Hey you! What d'you think you're doing?

BAR PATRONS Throw him out of here!
  – Why don't you just take off?
   – He's drunk! He's completely drunk!
    – Somebody call the cops!

SOPHIE How can you make these dreadful accusations?
Nathan! You are so wrong!

STINGO For pity's sake, leave her alone!
Just leave her alone!

BARMAN Cut it out! No brawling in this bar!

(Nathan takes hold of Sophie by the shoulders and shakes her in demented fury. Stingo and the Barman attempt to separate them.)

BAR PATRONS What's he doing to her?

NATHAN Did you cheat, connive, lay your sweet little ass –?

SOPHIE No! I never did such things, never in my life!
Please believe me, Nathan!

STINGO Nathan! I won't stand and watch another of your attacks.
Get away from her, do you hear?
Take your hands off – let her go!

BARMAN Leave the lady alone
and get the hell out of here!

BAR PATRONS Watch out! He's getting dangerous!
  – He's beating her up!
   – He's going to hurt her!
    – Hold him off!
     – He's gone completely crazy!

(Nathan throws Stingo to the floor. The Barman manages to retain his grip and keep Nathan away from Sophie.)

NATHAN Tell me, you Polish whore,
what did you do to protect yourself
while those millions died?
Can you tell me that?

(Nathan throws off the Barman, then storms out of the bar. Stingo tries to calm Sophie's despair.)

SOPHIE Hold me, Stingo, hold me!
Oh God, I feel so lost!
What am I going to do?
I'm so alone!

(Quick curtain)

ACT IV

Prologue

(The Narrator appears...)

NARRATOR   It was Sophie who told Nathan's brother Larry
of the terrible scene in the Maple Court Lounge
and of Nathan's disappearance.
Larry asked me to come and see him...

Scene 1

(The apartment of Larry Landau, Forest Hills, NY; early autumn 1947. The room is comfortably furnished, with well stocked bookcases, pictures on the walls, etc.)

LARRY   I don't have to tell you Nathan regards you very highly.
He's told me all about your work
and what a good writer he thinks you are.

STINGO   Well, he's the best literary critic I've ever met;
he's read *everything*.
I don't know how a research biologist would have the time...

LARRY *(quietly)*
Oh, Nathan has plenty of time for reading.
You see, he's not really a research biologist.
He's not even a bona-fide scientist –
he has no degree of any kind.
All that is a simple fabrication.

STINGO   I don't understand; do you mean –

LARRY *(gently)* I mean that this biology business
is my brother's masquerade –
a cover, nothing more than that.
He does have a job in the company library,
an undemanding sinecure, that's all. As you know,
Nathan is boundlessly bright, maybe even a genius.
He could have become almost anything
under the right circumstances.
But the truth is, my brother is quite mad.

STINGO   Oh, my God...

LARRY   Paranoid schizophrenia, or so the diagnosis goes.
Recently it's been aggravated
by the drugs he's been getting hold of...

STINGO   I see now... those rages...
It's all so hard to believe.
When he told me about Harvard –

LARRY   Oh, Nathan never went to Harvard.
He never went to any college
other than expensive funny farms.
No one knows about any of this,
least of all that sweet girl of his, Sophie.

STINGO   Oh, it's all so sad and awful...
Is there anything I can do?

LARRY	Yes. Keep an eye on him and report back to me from time to time. And if you could help him stay off the drugs…
STINGO	I'll try – if he ever reappears…
LARRY	Thanks…

(The scene fades…)

Scene 2

(The boarding house, Brooklyn; later the same day. As Stingo enters he encounters Yetta in a very agitated state.)

YETTA	Oh, Stingo, thank God you're here! While you were out Nathan telephoned. He sounded so crazy! He called Sophie terrible names to me – *terrible* names! I never heard such things in my life!
STINGO	Did she talk to him?
YETTA	She tried, but he refuses to speak with her. He was shouting and screaming all the time about you and Sophie… Stingo – he says he's coming for you! He thinks you and Sophie…
STINGO	Oh, my God… no!
YETTA	You want I call the police?
STINGO	No, wait – let me speak to Sophie first.

(As Stingo moves towards Sophie's door the phone on the hallway wall rings. Stingo picks up the receiver. From another part of the stage Nathan can be seen speaking into a phone.)

NATHAN *(mocking Southern accent)*
What's cookin', Sugar?
How's your hammer hangin'?

STINGO *(with forced heartiness)*
Nathan! It's good to hear from you!
How are you? *Where* are you?

NATHAN	We still gonna take that trip down south? You and me an' old Sophie?
STINGO	You bet! It's going to be the best trip ever –
NATHAN	We'll have a lot of free time, too, won't we?
STINGO	Why sure, all the time in the world…

NATHAN *(a rich chuckle)*
So I'll have the time to go off by myself
down there in New Orleans or Memphis,
leavin' *you* the free time to get you a little nooky, eh?

(Hearing Stingo speaking on the telephone Sophie comes out of her room. She stands by Stingo and tries to hear what Nathan is saying.)

STINGO   Well, Nathan, I expect we'll run into
a few friendly Southern girls –

NATHAN *(breaking in, and dropping the accent)*
    No, buddy, I don't mean Southern nooky!
    I mean *Polack* nooky!

STINGO *(dismayed)*
    Good God, Nathan...

NATHAN   I mean that when I'm out taking in the sights
    you and she are back at the Green Magnolia Hotel –
    and guess what you'll be doing!

SOPHIE   Here, let me speak to him.
    (taking the receiver from Stingo)
    Nathan, Nathan darling, listen to me –

NATHAN *(howling)*
    Get off the phone, you bitch!
    I never want to speak to you again, is that clear?

SOPHIE   Nathan –

NATHAN   D'you hear me – *get off the phone*!

(Trembling, Sophie hands the receiver back to Stingo.)

STINGO   Nathan, can we come and pick you up?

NATHAN   You wretched swine!
    You unspeakable creep!
    God damn you to hell for ever
    for betraying me behind my back –
    you whom I trusted like the best friend I ever had!
    And all the time you were in bed
    with the woman I was going to marry!

STINGO   It's not true –
    Nathan, *please*! Where are you?

(Nathan pulls out a pistol from his pocket and clicks off the safety catch.)

NATHAN   Not far away, old pal.
    In fact, I'm right around the corner.
    And I'm coming to get you treacherous scum.
    And then do you know what I'm going to do
    to you two deceitful, unspeakable pigs?
    Listen –

(He fires the pistol off close to the receiver. At the gun's report Stingo drops the telephone receiver in a panic and grabs Sophie's hand as they run towards the street door. Quick blackout.)

Interlude

(The Narrator appears...)

NARRATOR   We fled...
    Now, after the passing of time
    in this bloody century,
    whenever there has occurred
    any of those deeds of violence
    that has plundered our souls,
    my memory has turned back to Nathan,
    the poor lunatic whom I loved,

high on drugs and with a smoking barrel
in some nameless room or public booth.
His image has always seemed to foreshadow
those wretched years of madness
that were to follow, those unending years
of illusion, error, dream and strife.

But at that moment I felt only unutterable fear;
fear of Nathan and his merciless threat,
fear of the catastrophe barely avoided.
We became possessed, Sophie and I,
by a single-minded and terrible urge:
to flee Nathan and get as far away as possible.

We boarded a southbound train,
heading for my father's farm in Virginia.
We arrived in Washington
and took a room in a modest hotel...

Scene 3

(A hotel room in Washington; early autumn 1947. Sophie is sitting on the bed drinking whisky. She is edgy and preoccupied.)

SOPHIE   Stingo, where is telephone here?

STINGO   In the hallway downstairs.

SOPHIE   I want to call and find out about Nathan.
       I want to see if he is alright.

STINGO   Oh, Sophie, it's no use, there's nothing you can do.
       He was actually on the point of *killing us both*.
       Nathan is *insane*, Sophie! He has to be *locked up*.

SOPHIE   I just don't know how
       I'm going to face things without him...
       Maybe we could call Yetta at the house.
       She might be able to tell me if Nathan came back.

STINGO   Sophie, don't you see? It's all over.

(A strained silence. Sophie pours herself another drink.)

SOPHIE   Stingo, where are we going?

STINGO   To my father's farm I told you about,
       down in southern Virginia.
       Once we get settled –

SOPHIE   How do you mean 'get settled', Stingo dear?
       What's going to happen then?

STINGO   Sophie, I love you.
       I want us to be married...

SOPHIE   Oh, Stingo dear, when you mention getting married
       I get so full of trouble, so uncertain.
       Why don't we just go to the farm for a while and be together?
       We could decide about marriage later...

STINGO   Sophie, on our way down here,
       as you slept with your head on my shoulder,
       I allowed myself to dream.

I dreamed of a life shared with you,
and of waking every day to find your face beside me.

I dreamed of a house at peace, and of the company of friends;
I dreamed of a first-born on your knee and of our joy.
Sophie, I need you so very much.
Is it too much to hope you need me too?

SOPHIE *(very tenderly)*
Sweet Stingo, you're such a love.
You've cared for me in so many ways...

(She kisses him gently.)

STINGO   Sophie, darling...

SOPHIE   You know something, Stingo? I'm beyond thirty.
Someday I'll be old and ugly, and you'll still be quite young.
What would you do with an old lady like me?

STINGO   Sophie, stop tormenting me!

SOPHIE   No, Stingo, you need someone closer to your age
for your children, not someone like me.
Besides...

STINGO   ... Sophie?

SOPHIE   The doctors say I must be careful about having children
after all my sickness, after all that has happened to me...
(Sophie stares into the distance.)
Stingo, I must tell you something now
I've never told anyone before...
(Another pause...)
(softly)
On the day I arrived in Auschwitz,
it was beautiful.
The forsythia was in bloom...

(Fade to...)

Scene 4

(The rail station at Auschwitz-Birkenau, April 1, 1943. Late afternoon or early evening. The station platform is crowded with prisoners just descended from the train. A group of German officers and guards sort the prisoners into two lines. The camp Doctor and a young aide carrying a clipboard go slowly down the lines, inspecting the prisoners. The Doctor is visibly somewhat intoxicated, though managing to control himself. He is breathing heavily and has a film of perspiration on his face. He arrives at Sophie, who is waiting in line with her two children. The Doctor stops and scrutinises Sophie very carefully, insolently looking her up and down. He pays not the slightest attention to the children.)

DOCTOR *(in a quiet and even voice)*
You're very beautiful...
I'd like to get you in bed with me.
(Sophie nervously tries to avoid his gaze.)
I know you're a Polack,
but are you also one of those filthy Communists?

SOPHIE *(blurting out, terrified)*
> I'm Polish. Born in Cracow...
> I'm not Jewish! Or my children –
> they're not Jewish either.
> They're racially pure.
> They speak German.
> I'm Christian, a devout Catholic...

(The Doctor scrutinises her even more carefully.)

DOCTOR   So, you're not a communist...
You're a believer?

SOPHIE   *Ja, mein Hauptmann.*
I believe in Christ.

(The Doctor turns his back on her and murmurs something to the aide, who makes a note on the clipboard. Swaying almost imperceptibly, he turns back to Sophie.)

DOCTOR *(staring straight into Sophie's face)*
> So you believe in Christ the Redeemer?
> Did He not say 'Suffer the little children to come unto Me?'
(A strange pause...)
> *(quietly, in an almost offhand manner)*
> You may keep one of your children.

SOPHIE *(whispered)*
> *Bitte?*...

DOCTOR   You may keep one of your children.
The other will have to go.
Which one will you keep?

(The young aide looks incredulously at the Doctor.)

SOPHIE *(in a hollow voice)*
> You mean I have to choose?

DOCTOR   You're a Polack, not a Yid.
That gives you a privilege – a choice.

SOPHIE *(breaking down)*
> I can't choose! I can't!

DOCTOR   Shut up! Hurry now and choose.

SOPHIE *(beginning to scream)*
> Don't make me choose!

(Sophie is kneeling down, drawing the two children toward her.)

DOCTOR   Choose, goddammit, or I'll send them both over there.
(indicating the line of doomed prisoners)
Quick!

SOPHIE   Don't make me choose!
I can't choose!

DOCTOR *(to the aide)*
> Send them both over there, then –
> *nach links.*

(Blinded by desperate tears, Sophie pushes Eva away from her.)

SOPHIE *(crying out)*
>Take the baby!
>Take my little girl!

(Quite gently, the aide pulls Eva away from her mother, picks her up, and carries her off. The child cries out in terror.)

EVA   Mama! Mama!

(Sophie gives vent to a terrible, overwhelming scream of agony. The stage goes dark.)

Scene 5

(The hotel room in Washington. The room is full of the shadows of dusk. Stingo is staring at Sophie as if transfixed, unable to move.)

SOPHIE *(very softly)*
>In her arms she still carried her doll…
>In all these years since
>I have never been able to bear that word,
>or to speak it in any language…
(The evening light seems to dim further.)
>Suppose I had chosen Jan to go instead of Eva.
>Would that have changed anything?
>*(in a low, quiet voice)*
>Nothing would have changed anything…

(Overwhelmed by grief and memory, Sophie breaks down into a paroxysm of weeping. Stingo takes her into his arms and tries to comfort her. Eventually she calms down. Stingo kisses her gently… Sophie returns his caresses, and both become increasingly passionate. The scene dims…)

Interlude

(Morning sunlight fills the hotel room. Stingo wakes to find Sophie gone. There is a letter on the pillow. As he reads it, the voice of Sophie is heard. The scene gradually fades…)

SOPHIE   My Dearest Stingo – You're such a beautiful lover… I hate to leave. Forgive me for not saying Good-bye, but I must go back to Nathan. You must not think by this I am being cruel – I am so fond of you. But when I woke I was feeling so terrible and in despair about Nathan, so filled with guilt and thoughts of death, it was like ice flowing in my blood. So I must be with Nathan again for whatever that mean. I feel so bad, I must go now. Dearest Stingo, I may not see you again… you have meaned so much to me…

Scene 6

(The boarding house in Brooklyn, afternoon of the next day. Several police officers and ambulance men are gathered in the hallway. Yetta, ashen-faced and distraught, is being tended by some neighbours. Larry Landau is talking quietly to a policeman outside the door of Sophie's room. Stingo comes slowly into the house.)

YETTA *(weeping)*
>Oh Stingo, what a terrible thing
>they should do this to themselves…

LARRY *(to Stingo)*
>They didn't suffer. Cyanide pills.
>It was over in a few seconds…

(Stingo goes slowly into Sophie's room. Sophie and Nathan are lying peacefully in each other's arms on the bed. They are dressed in their nineteen-thirties clothes. Lying open in Nathan's hand is a book of Emily Dickinson poetry he had given Sophie. Stingo stands quietly by the bed for a moment, then gently takes up the book and glances at the open page.)

STINGO *(reading from the book at first)*

> 'Ample make this bed.
> Make this bed with awe;
> In it wait till judgement break
> Excellent and fair.
>
> Be its mattress straight
> Be its pillow round;
> Let no sunrise' yellow noise
> Interrupt this ground.'

(During Stingo's reading the Narrator appears. He joins with Stingo in declaiming the poem.)

STINGO and NARRATOR

> 'Ample make this bed.
> Make this bed with awe;
> In it wait till judgement break
> Excellent and fair.'

(The scene fades. All that remains visible is the figure of the Narrator.)

Epilogue

NARRATOR   And finally I wept…
I wept for Sophie and Nathan,
for Jan and Eva, and the brave Wanda.
My tears were a letting go of rage and sorrow
for all those who had become dear to me
and who now demanded my mourning;
the beaten, butchered, martyred
and betrayed children of the earth.

I once hoped to understand Auschwitz
through Sophie and all her contradictions.
I now know I never will…
'At Auschwitz, tell me, where was God?'
The response: 'Where was man?'

(The light slowly fades. Curtain)

End of opera